Fact Finders®

ENERGY REVOLUTION

WIND ENERGY

By M. M. Eboch

Consultant: Ellen Anderson
Executive Director of the Energy Transition Lab
Institute on the Environment
University of Minnesota, Twin Cities

CAPSTONE PRESS
a capstone imprint

Fact Finders Books are published by Capstone Press,
1710 Roe Crest Drive, North Mankato, Minnesota 56003
www.capstonepub.com

Library of Congress Cataloging-in-Publication Data
Names: Eboch, M. M., author.
Title: Wind energy / by M.M. Eboch.
Description: North Mankato, Minnesota : Fact Finders, an imprint of Capstone
    Press, [2019] | Series: Fact finders. Energy revolution | Includes
    bibliographical references and index. | Audience: Age 9. | Audience: Grades 4 to 6.
Identifiers: LCCN 2018040988 (print) | LCCN 2018042752 (ebook) |
ISBN 9781543555479 (eBook PDF) |
ISBN 9781543555417 (library binding) |
ISBN 9781543559071 (pbk.)
Subjects: LCSH: Wind power plants—Juvenile literature. | Wind power—Juvenile
literature. Classification: LCC TK1541 (ebook) | LCC TK1541 .E26 2019 (print) | DDC
333.9/2—dc23
LC record available at https://lccn.loc.gov/2018040988

Editorial Credits
Mandy Robbins, editor; Terri Poburka, designer; Jo Miller, media researcher;
Kathy McColley, production specialist

Photo Credits
Getty Images: KAZUHIRO NOGI/Staff, 27; Newscom: Prisma/Album, 4, Reuters/Sergio
Perez, 26, ZUMA Press/Ryumin Alexander, 28; Shutterstock: airphoto.gr, 7, Arturo Limon,
14-15, Jitloac, 8-9, Jordi C, 24, juerginho, 22, Kris Wiktor, 11, majeczka, Cover, Mattis
Kaminer, 13, remymatins, 25, Stockr, 20-21, Third key, 18, Tony Moran, 16-17, Vadim Orlov,
29, YAKOBCHUK VIACHESLAV, 23, Yann hubert, 21 (inset); Wikimedia: unknown/public
domain, 19

Design Elements
Shutterstock: HAKKI ARSLAN, T.Sumaetho

TABLE OF CONTENTS

CHAPTER 1

WIND POWER THROUGH THE AGES

Open a window and a breeze may help cool your house. But wind can also create enough power to turn on your lights. Wind power is **renewable** energy. It can take the place of the traditional **power plants** that make energy. It may seem like wind energy is something new. But it is actually very old. Wind has been used to power sailboats for at least 7,000 years. Wind fills the sail and pushes the boat.

Later people built windmills to harness the wind's power. A windmill is a tower with blades rotating around the top. These blades work like a boat's sails. The wind pushes them and makes them turn. They then turn a **shaft** inside the windmill. This turns the wind's energy into motion energy.

Windmills were common in Europe starting in the 1100s. People used them to grind grain or pump water. These early windmills only worked on days with strong winds. They could not store energy for later use. The energy could be used only inside the windmill. It could not be sent to nearby homes.

. . . .

renewable—describes power from sources that you can use over and over again that cannot be used up, such as wind, water, and the sun

power plant—a building or group of buildings used to create electricity

shaft—a rotating bar that transmits motion

By the end of the 1800s, people had figured out how to make electricity in power plants. Windmills could only power what was directly attached to them. Power plants could make electricity and send it along wires into homes and businesses. When the electricity reached these buildings, it could be used in many ways. Windmills were still used to pump water. But for electricity, people turned to power plants.

Today we depend on electricity in our lives. It makes lights turn on. It can run heaters or air conditioners. It can charge phones and run computers. Imagine life with no electricity!

How Electricity Is Created

boiler

turbine

generator

steam

burner

electricity

Fossil fuels produce almost 63 percent of the United States' energy.

Any type of fuel can be used to make electricity in power plants. Most power plants use coal, oil, or gas as fuel. Burning these **fossil fuels** creates heat. The heat boils water, which creates steam. The hot steam moves through the air and spins a **turbine**. The turbine runs a **generator** that makes electricity.

fossil fuel—fuel, including coal, oil, or natural gas, made from the remains of ancient organisms

turbine—a machine driven by water, steam, or gas passing through the blades of a wheel and making it revolve

generator—a machine that produces electricity by turning a magnet inside a coil of wire

GETTING ENERGY FROM THE WIND

People need to start finding renewable fuel sources for many reasons. Burning fossil fuels creates **pollution**. Pollution adds to climate change, which causes rising sea levels and extreme weather. In addition to the problem of pollution, we may begin to run out of fossil fuel in as little as 30 years. Once coal and oil are taken from the ground, they are gone. If we run out, we'll need other ways to make electricity. Fortunately wind, water, sunlight, and the earth's internal heat never run out. These forms of energy are renewable. Renewable energy causes less pollution.

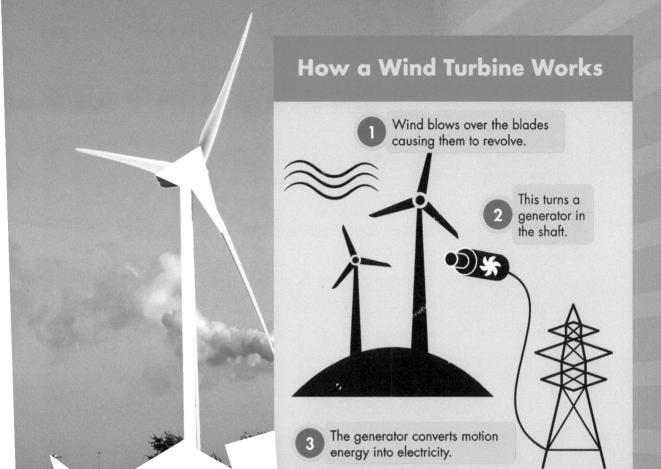

How a Wind Turbine Works

1 Wind blows over the blades causing them to revolve.

2 This turns a generator in the shaft.

3 The generator converts motion energy into electricity.

So how do we turn wind into electricity? We go back to the windmill. A wind power plant works like any other power plant. But it does not need to burn fuel. The wind itself turns the turbine blades. Then the blades run the generator to create electricity. A small windmill can power one home, business, or farm. Large wind farms can provide power to up to 1 million homes. They are called farms because they "harvest" the wind.

pollution—harmful materials that damage the environment

HOW WIND TURBINES WORK

Modern windmills that make electricity are called wind turbines. They convert wind power into electricity. The electricity can be stored or sent long distances. Today wind provides power to millions of homes and businesses.

Modern wind turbines may have towers more than 300 feet (90 meters) tall. Wind blows faster at higher **altitudes**. In addition, wind is less bumpy high in the air. Tall towers reach this fast, smooth-flowing wind.

Wind power works best where the winds are strong and steady. When the wind is not blowing, no new power is made. Then **batteries** can help. Batteries store extra power when the wind is strong. When the wind stops blowing, the batteries can send out their stored power.

Today wind turbines usually have only three blades. One blade would actually harness the most wind power. But one or two blades would be unstable. The blades would wobble and put **stress** on the structure. Using three blades keeps the wind turbine stable. Using more blades would slow the turbine.

....

altitude—how high a place is above sea level
battery—a container holding chemicals that store and create electricity
stress—the physical pressure, pull, or other force on an object

FACT

The biggest wind turbines are more than 850 feet (260 m) tall. Each blade can be 350 feet (107 m) long.

WIND ENERGY TODAY

Today's wind farms have hundreds of wind turbines. The turbines might be spread out over hundreds of miles. In between, the land can be used for growing food, grazing cattle, or other purposes.

Wind power is most popular in Europe and Asia. It makes up almost 12 percent of the electricity in the 28 countries that make up the European Union. Worldwide, the United Kingdom makes the most wind power, followed by Germany and China.

Wind energy does not yet provide much of the United States' energy. Wind provides 5 percent of energy in the United States. Texas produces the most wind power of any state. It gets 13 percent of its electricity from wind. Iowa is a much smaller state, but it generates more than 31 percent of its electricity from wind.

The use of wind energy is growing around the world. According to a study done at Harvard University, wind could supply more than 40 times the electricity the world needs.

Magdeburg, Germany, is the site of one of the country's many wind farms.

PROBLEMS AND POTENTIAL WITH WIND POWER

Wind energy causes less pollution than using fossil fuels. But it requires a lot of money, planning, and construction. And even then, wind energy can be problematic in some ways.

BAD NEWS FOR BIRDS AND BATS

Birds and bats can crash into wind turbines and die. The Altamont Pass wind farm in California is the oldest wind farm in the United States. Its planners didn't realize that they were building turbines in a busy path where birds of prey fly. More than 1,000 owls, eagles, hawks, and falcons are killed there each year. Owners are taking steps to lessen this problem. They stop the turbines occasionally, and they are replacing the old turbines with new ones. These new turbines have a safer design for birds.

Most bird and bat deaths that are caused by wind turbines can be prevented. First, wind farms must be put in the right place. They should avoid the main bird migration routes. **Radar** can also help. It can tell when large birds are near. Then the turbines can be slowed or shut down. High-pitched sounds can drive away bats. Bats are most active when wind speeds are low. To save bats, the turbines can be stopped when winds are slow.

radar—a device that uses radio waves to track the location of objects

USING SEA BREEZES

As wind blows over land, it loses strength when it hits mountains and valleys. Offshore wind has more power and blows more steadily. This makes oceans a great place for wind farms. These wind farms can make more power because of the stronger winds. Many countries with coasts have offshore wind farms.

Offshore wind farms do have some problems. It is not easy to build in the ocean. That means it costs more. People may worry about harm to sea animals and birds. But some studies show that offshore wind farms are safe for birds. The towers may even act as fake **reefs**. This can bring more fish into the area.

reef—an underwater strip of rocks, coral, or sand near the surface of the ocean

Using the Wind at Sea

Offshore wind farms are not yet common, but numbers are growing. Europe has at least 17 ocean wind farms in 11 countries. The United Kingdom and Germany use the most offshore wind. China is third.

The United States has almost 100,000 miles (160,934 kilometers) of coastline. About 39 percent of people live near the coast. Offshore wind farms could be a big energy source. One commercial offshore wind farm was completed by 2018. It is off the coast of Rhode Island. More than 25 more are being planned. Most will be on the East Coast. The Great Lakes may be another good site for offshore wind farms.

PLANNING WIND FARMS

Wind farms can be safe for animals on land or at sea. But each place is different. Planners must study the site. They must predict how wind turbines will affect animals. Then workers have to watch wind farms to check for problems.

Some people are still against wind farms. Studies show that wind farms do not affect human health. But some people may not like the sound and vibration from the spinning blades. Other people don't like the way the farms look. They may think the turbines will ruin their view of the countryside. Often wind farm companies try to build away from most people.

The wide-open countryside is a great place for wind farms.

The First Electric Windmill

In 1888, Charles F. Brush built the first large windmill to make electricity. The 60-foot (18-m) tall iron tower stood in his backyard in Ohio. The windmill had 144 wooden blades. Its wheel was 56 feet (17 m) across. The spinning wheel turned pulleys and belts. They were connected to more than 400 batteries. This windmill powered hundreds of lamps and three electric motors.

THE FUTURE OF WIND ENERGY

Wind could supply all the power the world needs. But will it?

Most wind farms in use today are small. Sometimes they work along with fossil fuel power plants. Wind farms might not provide enough power for everyone. But they can help.

Some changes may make wind power more useful. New wind turbines might be larger. They could have longer, lighter blades. This means they would be more **efficient**. They could be used in less windy areas.

....

efficient—the quality of not wasting time or energy

Inspired by Nature

One day Dr. Frank E. Fish saw a sculpture of a humpback whale. He thought the artist put the bumps on the wrong side of the flipper. Engineers thought the front edges of fins should be smooth. But humpback whales really do have bumps on the front edges of their fins. How could that work? Dr. Fish and other scientists tried some tests. They were  surprised by the results. Air pulls hard against a smooth blade with a very steep angle. That pull could stop a turbine motor. Adding bumps lets blades work at a steeper angle, which is more efficient. This discovery led to the development of new wind turbines in the early 2000s. They can make 20 percent more power.

WIND ENERGY ENGINEERING

Larger wind turbines make more energy than small ones. Keeping these big machines working is hard. The wind can damage them. People making wind farms need to know how wind affects the turbines. Wind is always changing direction and strength. High winds can put stress on parts of the wind turbine.

The stress of extreme weather can destroy a wind turbine.

Engineers build models of turbines to learn what works best.

A wind farm needs engineers. Engineers design and build machines and keep them working. They also search for ways to make better machines. Engineers choose the right materials for the wind turbines. They must know the strength and weight of the material. Engineers must also know how much it costs and how long it will last. The turbines must stand up to high winds, snow, and ice. They may even need to withstand earthquakes. Engineers may try new materials or different designs to withstand challenges.

It would not be safe to build a wind turbine and wait to see what happens. Engineers must predict what will happen. To do this, they use computer models. These models show how a thing may work in the real world.

TROUBLESHOOTING TURBINES

Planning well before building a wind farm is important, but the challenges do not end there. Engineers may find a problem they did not expect. Then they need to adapt.

Workers monitor turbines for signs of damage. Each turbine has many **sensors**. These sensors send an alert if something is wrong. They may even stop the turbine for safety. It is best to find problems early. Then parts can be fixed before they fail. The turbine can keep running to provide power.

To repair wind turbines, cranes lift workers up to the turbine.

Sensors can also show how well the turbines are working. The sensors can even make changes to keep the turbines working at their best.

Each blade has separate controls. This helps balance the forces so the blades do not get too much stress. With this control, turbines can use larger blades to capture more energy.

. . . .

sensor—a device that detects and reports on input such as heat and pressure

Regular maintenance keeps turbines working well.

IS YOUR FUTURE IN WIND?

Do you want to help the world use more wind energy? Does designing and building wind farms sound interesting? Then you might want to study engineering. You could find better ways to use wind power.

Engineers continually design new wind turbines. A group of engineers in Germany is combining wind with waterpower. A Japanese scientist designed a typhoon turbine. It could harness the enormous energy in tropical storms. In Alaska, a wind turbine floats in the air like a giant balloon. It takes advantage of the strong wind currents in the air. One new design doesn't have blades at all. It is shaped like a giant straw to capture swirling wind. This design is safer for birds and bats.

Researchers in Spain created a tube turbine.

Prepare for an Engineering Career

Engineers need to have a background in math and science. They may also study computers and robots. Many schools and communities have math, science, and robotics clubs. Get involved! Working in groups can also help you learn great teamwork skills. Engineers often work together to solve problems.

Engineers in Japan have created a bladeless turbine.

MANY WAYS TO GET INVOLVED

Maybe you're interested in wind power, but you don't dream of being an engineer. You can find many other ways to work in the wind energy field. No matter your interests, there is a job there to suit you. Factory workers build all the pieces that make up wind turbines. There are about 8,000 parts in each turbine. Special scouts look for good land to build wind farms. They seek out wide-open spaces that get lots of wind. Scientists must decide if a site will work and be safe for animals. Construction workers put together the pieces that are made in factories to build the wind farms that engineers design.

A worker in Gelderland, Netherlands, helps assemble a turbine.

The work doesn't end there. Many people are needed to keep a wind farm running. Some people fix damaged wind turbines. These brave workers are called skyworkers. They climb the wind turbine towers with a web of ropes and safety harnesses. They inspect, clean, and repair the blades.

Wind power and other renewable energy sources are growing. This will help us power our homes for years to come. Could you play a part in supplying the energy of the future?

Installing wind turbines once they are built requires heavy machinery.

GLOSSARY

altitude (AL-ti-tood)—how high a place is above sea level

battery (BA-tuh-ree)—a container holding chemicals that store and create electricity

efficient (uh-FI-shuhnt)—the quality of not wasting time or energy

fossil fuel (FAH-suhl FYOOL)—fuel, including coal, oil, or natural gas, made from the remains of ancient organisms

generator (JEN-uh-ray-tur)—a machine that produces electricity by turning a magnet inside a coil of wire

pollution (puh-LOO-shuhn)—harmful materials that damage the environment

power plant (POW-ur PLANT)—a building or group of buildings used to create electricity

radar (RAY-dar)—a device that uses radio waves to track the location of objects

reef (REEF)—an underwater strip of rocks, coral, or sand near the surface of the ocean

renewable (ri-NOO-uh-buhl)—describes power from sources that you can use over and over again that cannot be used up, such as wind, water, and the sun

sensor (SEN-sur)—a device that detects and reports on input such as heat and pressure

shaft (SHAFT)—a rotating bar that transmits motion

stress (STRESS)—the physical pressure, pull, or other force on an object

turbine (TUR-bine)—a machine driven by water, steam, or gas passing through the blades of a wheel and making it revolve

READ MORE

Felix, Rebecca. *Wind Energy.* Earth's Energy Resources. Minneapolis: Abdo Pub., 2018.

Grady, Colin. *Wind Energy.* Saving the Planet Through Green Energy. New York: Enslow Publishing, 2017.

Morlock, Theresa. *Wind Farms: Harnessing the Power of Wind.* Powered Up!: A STEM Approach to Energy Sources. New York: PowerKids Press, 2018.

INTERNET SITES

Use FactHound to find Internet sites related to this book.

Visit www.facthound.com

Just type in 9781543555417 and go.

 Super-cool stuff! Check out projects, games and lots more at **www.capstonekids.com**

CRITICAL THINKING QUESTIONS

1. We use electricity in many ways. How many ways can you think of? What would life be like without electricity?

2. Wind farms can hurt animals. What is one way that humans can avoid causing harm when their energy needs are in conflict with nature?

3. Some people don't like the way wind farms look. How might engineers address this?

INDEX